DANDELIONS:MULTIVERSE OF POEMS-VOLUME 2

MUHAMED FARHAAN

We firstly dedicate this book to Almighty God

To our family and Friends

Contents

Contents

Preface

The word dandelions is compared to poets here.

An anthology where poets express themselves through beautiful poems.

Indeed a multiverse of poems.

Presenting you 'DANDELIONS: MULTIVERSE OF POEMS'

A two volume anthology

2/2 Penned by 30 writers

Acknowledgements

To all my co- authors

Abirami Vetriselvan

Poornima Kamatchi.P

Mahlu Made-Me

Shakil kalam

Sharmistha Gupta

Ken gokdman

Amd.Maid Corbic

Shakil Ahmed

Egor

Olatubosun David

Arun Hariharan

Ruth M Martz

Nishanthini Iniyan

Andrew Huang

Sanhita Sinha

Bilkis Moola

Nivedha V

Fariel Shafee

Afrah Sadiqa S S

Jhenson Tyrone Villena

Bhavya M Bhaskaran

Shravani Prakashchandra

LaVern Spencer McCarthy

ACKNOWLEDGEMENTS

Maja Milojkoviç

Aayush Aggarwal

Nivedha Somasundharam

Suk Raj Darjee

Neelam Lashari

Sai Sravanthi

Eity Mithila

1. Hold on

We survive so much
We rarely live
Life is brittle
All moments,All memories
Aren't little
Time passes
We will one day
Turn carcasses
Ding Dong
Life shouldn't be long
It should be large
Past is gone
Tomorrow will be a new dawn
Today hold on
Just hold on
Hold on
Days have been cold
Nights have been old
Lost so much
It's difficult to gain
Tears flow more than
November rain

It's been hard to talk
Almost nothing to say
Life has been shades of grey
We had triggers enough
Life has been tough
Past is gone
Tomorrow will be a new dawn
Today hold on
Just hold on
Hold on
©Muhamed Farhaan

2. Life in an aquarium

We see through our tiny eyes,
Beyond the glass barrier,
Creatures scarier.
They aren't rude,
Give us satisfying food.
We swim through the tunnels , colourful stones, and bubbles,
Without causing any kind of troubles.
We see these mysterious creatures laugh,
Capture memories with us in a photograph.
We do have emotions,
We have dreams to settle in ponds and oceans.
We also do feel ok when these creatures come to visit us,
Without much fus.
Our life is full of thrills,
Will keep existing till we have functioning gills.
©Muhamed Farhaan

3. Volcano

Times there , when I used to say yes for everything
People took me for a hell of a ride
Because all their rules, I abide
Now I have learnt to say no
Erupting like a Volcano
I have changed my path
Full of Wrath
Time to break all the shackles and locks with a new key,
With all injustice done to me
I have fire burning in my eyes
Which cannot tolerate anymore lies
I'm no sage
Breaking my cage
Full of Rage
I have learned to say no
Erupting like a Volcano
People didn't expect me in this anger
Didn't expect this banger
They know me with silence
Not this violence
Despite the pain
I have got a balance to maintain

MUHAMED FARHAAN

Not being insane
For every scorching heat there is rain
©Muhamed Farhaan

• 5 •

Compiler's Bio

Farhaan is a dental student currently doing his internship from Thai moogambigai dental college and hospital ,Chennai. He also holds an Diploma in Modern Applied Psychology from Achology ,and also pursuing Sports Dentistry from Institute of Sports Science and Technology(IIST), Pune. He has compiled 9 anthologies and co-authored 16 of them.You can follow his write ups on instagram @anonymoussoul23 and also on allpoetry/ anonymoussoul23VRV

4. The Rhyme of Life

Every life dawns from a single cell,
Protected in the womb; a sacred dwell.
The mother knows not, her child;
Yet her zeal lays revived.
Two souls which never met,
Synchronize like a cornet.
Then soars the time, so does the rhyme.
Life takes a new turn, a walk through the verne.
A truth that cannot be denied,
No two roads are ever tied.
Life is but a sail, over the troughs and crests;
So ride not with gruff but zest.
Everyone's been gifted a strength;
To glean their way and walk their length.
Life holds out its hand,
Exhorting us to join its band.
So never put a blame;
Let your hand grasp the fame.
As a brook steals its banks,
So does life decree a rank.
Some walk wise, while vice walks some;
Hurdles are to be fought, never be distraught.

Life is all about splice.
And so wafts the Rhyme Of Life.

<u>Poem by Abirami Vetriselvan</u>

<u>BIO:</u> *Abirami Vetriselvan, a dental practitioner by profession, having penned down case reports and summaries, has been hit with an interest towards literature wandering from a factual world to a fantasy based reality.*

5. I anticipate your return

Holding your hands in Eventide,
Surfing on the notes of your flute,
Feeling the cuddle , near high tides,
Is the moment, when I be jubilant .
I lost my blemish ,
when I sleep on your femoris,
Autumn preaches me the various colors,
About your amour, my love.
Suddenly my attire is like the Queen,
When you play the lullaby,
Hearing your angelic voice with keen,
I Adore my strength.
Alas! You are invisible, after a nap,
I wanna reach you,
How will I do???
I wanna feel ur cuddle,
When will it happen???
I wanna be your sparkle,
Without getting Sinked,
Into the ocean of illusion,
And Want to feel your dimensions.

I wanna feel your pulse,
Wanna know your magic,
Wanna go beyond the universe,
But how and when ?
I know it's a tough journey,
And I know only u can accompany me,
In this eternal voyage to Paradise,
Where I become rhapsodic.
Wanna be your kid,
And remain as your Princess,
Wanna be with your identity,
Because I know only that never change...
___Poem by Poornima Kamatchi P___

6. He is the reason

I cry, cry, cry,
Without knowing the reason- why,
His garlands reaches my eyes,
And shoots my fear, through his gaze till the sky,
Axiomatically, I don't want to leave him.
I fall, fall, fall,
For his luminescent lovely heart,
Where my nerves rest in peace, hearing his propulsion,
And my soul gets showered by his sandal wood perfume,
Axiomatically, I don't want to leave him.
I blink, blink ,blink,
Near the dark fire of wheels,
Whirling for his heavenly grin,
Because he fetches me the unaccountable platonic love,
Axiomatically, I don't want to leave him.
I search, search, search,
Inside the clouds filled with puzzles,
Yes it's his iconic fruity voice,
Which I hear in my dreams, in paradise,
Axiomatically, I don't want to leave him.
I crave, crave, crave,
To stay with my redeemer, perpetually,

And get lost in his golden words,
By sailing in his contemplation eternally,
Axiomatically, I don't want to leave him.
I hold, hold ,hold
His legacy, the celestial Empire,
In my charming planet,
Which Made him to adore his princess,
Axiomatically, I don't want to leave him.
I walk, walk ,walk
Around his triangles of dandelions,
But his sweet meticulosity with Amor,
Was the vivacious pillar for my soul,
Axiomatically, I don't want to leave him.
We dance, dance ,dance,
On the ring of stars and tulips,
Where his vibrant existence and omnipresence,
Was known to me ,after ages,
Axiomatically, he don't want to leave me..
Poem by Poornima Kamatchi P

7. This is the time

This is the time,
That I should see only your eyes,
To change myself into the dye,
And paint your glamour in my walls.
This is the time,
That I should feel only your breath,
To vindicate myself from the guilt,
By tasting your quotes.
This is the time,
That I should hear only your voice,
That quenches my desires,
And holds the ultimate energy.
This is the time,
That I should love you more,
Want to feel your touch,
Through the air, water, earth, fire and atmosphere.
This is the time,
That I should also understand your love,
The way you feel me,
And your anxiety , to protect me.
This is the time,
To feel Your crystal clear ,pure tears for me,

Your smile, plans , care and responsibility,
And your time for my welfare.
As this is the time,
To see your gaze,
Through the sun rays in the dawn,
And your charm in moon light.
That this is the time,
To not to leave your golden petals,
While dancing in the ball room,
And trust you , without turmoil.
Will you bless me?
That I should continue to be your lover,
And have the yearning for you,
By not forgetting you even in my reverie.
Will you articulate yourself?
Again in my dreams,
Will you appear in front of me?
My creator and life holder…
I know that through the air,
You break my hardships,
And feed the love day and night.
But I am waiting for the time,
That takes us closer and closer,
And to love you better and better, than yesterday,
To swipe my life towards your way…
I expect a lot from you,
But you never do it,

And teach me the depth of pure love,
In this world of sanctity..
I feel this is the time,
To learn the classics from you,
That you and I , eye to eye,
Share the tremendous energy , ever lasting..
This is the time,
I feel your glowing manliness, an amour,
So called armor, that makes me unbreakable,
While sailing in the maelstrom.
This is the time
I realized you are the only treasure,
Only man in my life,
Who swims always ,inside deep ocean of my heart......
Poem by Poornima Kamatchi P

Dr.Poornima Kamatchi.P, BDS,is from Chennai, Tamil Nadu,India. Currently doing her internship in Thai moogambigai dental College and hospital. She is proud and happy to be as a dental surgeon .Her hobbies are travelling and reading. She is the co-author of anthologies like my Chennai ,food, music my medicine ,bon voyage -an international anthology, lights in the darkness, bicycle and tempus machine,laconic tales...

8. A Dandelion's Wish

I wanna be a child
I wanna blow away,
on a dandelion's wish,
into the pages of a fairytale
Dwindling through the muse of change,
in its last epony,
as I am swarmed with
butterflies with silver wings,
guiding me through no man's land
Oh, to be free
Floating in the clouds
Poem by Mahlu Made-Me

BIO: *Mahlu Made-Me, born and raised in the Netherlands, always had a heart for reading and writing. During her literature study in Belgium, the spark was lit by her poetry classes given by the best professor of the entire campus. After a lot of turbulence, she decided to give space to that flame. Now she is a new writer diving into the world of poetry, making a debut on Allpoetry.*

9. The Poetry of Immortal Love

Kayes devoted himself in love, in this colourful day.

He saw Laila Bint Mahadi in a school;

She is like a piece of diamond-pearl

Scattered in the haystack.

Her body is scenic sticky as like Cypress tree.

Her eyes were like a maya deer,

Her one sight would tear thousands of

Hearts in an instant. The twinkling of her deep black eyes

Could make a thousand hearts storm.

In Laila's eye-sight may the whole world be destroyed.

Her alluring appearance; like the moon in the sky of Arabia.

When she snatched the human heart,

She was like a marvellous fairy of Persia.

Her face was as bright as a lamp with thick black hair.

Her 'night'; name has been successful with crow-like black hair.

Layla's voice is heard in the cuckoo's voice;

Then I think, is that possible! How it can be so beautiful

Someone's voice? Then the sun also rises in the west-

Yes, it's possible! The milk that Laila sips, so be it

Turned pink by the touch of her lips. Lucky;

Who is the lucky man! The eyes of lust
Whose house will the girl go to! Will illuminate that house.
Not even that little mole on her pink cheek;
Than anything in the whole world; Beautiful?
Impossibly beautiful! Cloudless silver moons' sky.
Deep darkness has come down to Layla's fate.
She had to tie up a family with that old man
The sky, the wind, the forest were bewildered by that sorrow
Plants. Kayes become 'Majnu'; disoriented human being.
Kayes is in love with Layla, Layla is in love with Kayes,
Kayes has gone crazy; known by the name of 'Majnu' in this
world
Writes poems for Layla and walks around the streets.
Wants to recite poetry, no one listens to his satire -
When he was pushed away blaming as crazy, he came again to
express him
Majnu's days are spent in such misery; the day is over.
He wanders in the forest, in his own mind
Talks to the beast. Lifeless, dull voices.
Laila became mad with the grief of her old husband.
One day news came to Majnu's ear in a listless wind,
Laila has left this worldly affection, to the address of hereafter.
Majnu rushes like crazy to Layla's grave,
The weeping Majnu's soul left the body.
Is it possible to draw a picture of such love at any time?
** NB: Written in the light of the life story of the immortal love*
story "Layla-Majnu" in the Arabic novel.

Poem by SHAKIL KALAM

Root Finder Writer Shakil Kalam was born on December 3, in Feni district in Bangladesh. He received two Master's Degree in Governance Studies from University of Dhaka. He has completed a diploma course on IAS and IFRS from the Institute of Chatered Accountants of Bangladesh (ICAB). Mostly, he is renowned as Central Banker, Corporate Governance Specialist, Researcher, Poet, Translator as well as Child-Litterateur. Now engaged in a research foundation as a Honourary research fellow and consultant at financial sectors. Recently he achieved "Order of Shakespeare Medal- 2021" and "Gujarat Sahittya Academy Award-2021" which were initiated by world's most active writers forum Motivational Strips as well as awarded by the Humanity for the Sake of God, World Welfare Council's prize

"Global Prestigious Award-2021" on the eve of Gandhi Joyanti 2021. He is the International Ambassador for the Chamber of Writers and Artists in Spain as well as member of International English literary journal's advisory board of "ENGLIT" and "Unending Quest." He is also the members of Dhaka University Political Science and Master in Governance Studies Alumni Association.

10. Fingers talk

Sequinned strokes in lithe hands hover
rummage streaming sun over creamy latte-

Piano keys rustle in tumbling fever
basking in the heat of fragile fingers-

Juvenile hands dream articulate
yearn artistry in poise-

Fissured gold ring clasped my agile finger
and I sashay in sublime touch-

Alabaster hands trail in porcelain gown
gripped in fever down the aisle-

Fleshy paintbrushes colour your eyes gentle
nestle passionate kisses upon iris pure-

Groovy fingers nailed in solitude
croon slices on canvas rare-
Poem by Sarmistha Gupta

Sarmistha Gupta has been creating Petey in genres that fascinate her. Since childhood the manifestation of life in abundant flavours evolving through poetry has had its influence on her and she uses it as her tool for meaningful expression.She writes under the pen name of Ninkasi and she tries to weave a gamut of ideas in an alluring tapestry of art.

11. Titleless

She hid from Death but he found her hiding inside her youth.
And when he came he took her aside and whispered,
"So how was it, your life?"
And she told him , "I'll let you know when I am done.
I have not yet flown like a firefly nor kissed a handsome prince.
And I would enjoy a walk along the Seine."
She argued for a handful of her dreams.
But in the end he took them all.
<u>Poem by Ken Gokdman</u>

Ken Goldman, former Philadelphia teacher of English and Film
Studies, is an Active member of the Horror Writers Association.
He has homes on the Main Line in Pennsylvania and at the
Jersey shore. His stories have appeared in over 935 independent

press publications in the U.S., Canada, the UK, and Australia with over twenty due for publication in 2021. Since 1993 Ken's tales have received seven honorable mentions in The Year's Best Fantasy & Horror. He has written six books : three anthologies of short stories, YOU HAD ME AT ARRGH!! (Sam's Dot Publishers), DONNY DOESN'T LIVE HERE ANYMORE (A/ A Productions) and STAR-CROSSED (Vampires 2); and a novella, DESIREE, (Damnation Books). His first novel OF A FEATHER (Horrific Tales Publishing) was released in January 2014. SINKHOLE, his second novel, was published by Bloodshot Books August 2017.

12. Stay Gold

In my opinion Bangtan's most beautiful Music video,
It's representation of tiny little cues and moments are brilliant
I felt like the music video represented our memorable quarantine
days versus our normal days
We all were stuck in different places and our emotions also were
captured in one place
The music video represented our cold pandemic days were we
missed ourselves and our surroundings
On the other hand it shows how happy we were during the pre
pandemic and enjoyed beautiful sunshine
The Music video also showcases on how we missed the original
sunshine and sunshine in ourselves too
The gold sprinkles represent the gold memories and aura we still
have left
It represents our hope
The music video further says that situation and our way of living
during pandemic days might have changed but still we could
find happiness in small things and stay gold, it shows we can still
look forward to a beautiful future.

Any BTS have incorporated some of their memorable moments
to further beautify the already marvellous music video
Stay gold is a hope to everyone
It is a message to stay strong and stay gold with your thoughts
Thanks a Trillion to Bangtan for this
© <u>Nivedha V</u>

Nivedha is a dental student from Chennai. Her major part of life is juggling between BDS and BTS , coz they are the coz of her euphoria..Her other hobbies are playing keyboard, baking , reading books and to be a better soul everyday .

13. Halloween In My Land

I still feel present in everything.
I am someone who loves love.
But I also want to feel the fear again.
When other people create things
The kind I don't hope for
The point of it all is to be angry with Halloween.
But I know the fear is justified.
Only if I meet some vampires around me
Because I'm someone who loves tea.
Every day to feel that day
I want to get various sweets
And I don't feel guilty about anything.
If sometimes someone doesn't throw me off the horizon
Because I am someone who only dreams.
To continue to be all that I am and am not
I dream of love still living in me
To share good and evil with everyone
Because I want to offer my costume
Like Batman flying the world
Just to keep building my dreams
May love continue to live in me
This night will be memorable for sure.

Because I only hope for one
Yes, love will continue to live in me.
As long as I'm still alive!
Poem by Amb. Maid Corbic

Maid Corbic from Tuzla, Bosnia and Herzegovina. He has 22 years and his spare time he writes poetry that repeatedly praised as well as rewarded. He also selflessly helps others around him, and he is moderator of the World Literature Forum WLFPH (World Literature Forum Peace and Humanity) for humanity and peace in the world in Bhutan.

14. Living Paradise

You have potential enough to fly crossing the skyline
To touch the yawning stars of cerulean sky
To build an oasis with billion emeralds
Surpassing the glow of twilight waning moon
Where mystic roses bloom like the land of wonders
You have spirit enough to lit fire of blessed light
Removing the hellish gloom of thousand seamy years
Annihilating vile lies of countless decadent years
Raise your spirit like violent storms of rainy season
To spread your exalted thoughts over the dormant universe
Don't lose heart before the lies of ebbing eons
Enunciated by the evil prowls of ancient days
Tell them you are powerful like an angel of gorgeous paradise
You can make impossible possible with your tenacious nature
Your hidden beauty lies in strong resolution.
Don't be like men or women of filthy ignorance
Who are tired before dreaming the dream of paradise
By virtue of your efforts you can make a paradise
Transforming fiendish pain into a soothing pleasure
Where beauty of life never declines like withering flowers.
Your unspoken words in this crowded world
May change the world in wink of eyes

Your inmost feelings amid the infinite realities
Can create a huge epoch in the dwindling world
Bliss of life may drip from your cute lips.
Poem by Shakil Ahmed

Enter Caption

15. Dandelion is my favourite flower

Dandelion is my favourite flower,
(although i love wild roses as well)
because the domestic dandelion is swell with the adding of flour,
i can make dumplings with dandelion petals and escape my
personal beriberi hell!
Dandelion is my favourite flower
(although i love bluebells too)
because If you've escavated the soil, having found the roots
You can brew some top-qiality coffee which You can easily boil
the rich aroma and the wonderful taste to boot!
Dandelion is my favourite flower
(although i love carnations, in addition to it)
because two thousand domestic dandelion flowers
(If you've equipped yourself as a dandelion plower)
are the very ammunition you need to make forty liters of
sparkling, orange-juice-coloured wine which come into fruition
and turn to effervescent, festive showers and shine!
<u>Poem by Egor</u>

His name is Egor. He is 28 years old. He lives in Belarus all his life. Even as a child he loved to read voraciously, he has been studying the English language since 5 years of age. He finished the local school where his teacher Ludmila Dainakova Nikolaevna taught him 'this language of angels' on a more profound level. Then he entered Minsk State Linguistic University where he discovered a passion for scribbling down poems in his free time and leisure time - a passion which has stayed (although fluctuated from time to time due various life issues) all of his life

16. Tunes of a Raining Day

When night births the dawn
Young and meek, the sun peeps
A witness and guide to its path
Breeze is gentle and soothing
Conveying the creator's mind
And blessing to mankind.
Like a newborn
Tears of joy from the heavens drizzled
Cooling the verdant meadows
And the landscapes.
Distant hills amidst the fog emerged.
Like smoke into the thin air;
The mist dissolves and fades.
Streams in a gentle flow,
And birds in the early glee,
Heading towards their diverse destinations.
The firmament sings the tunes of a raining day:
In this rumbling of thunder;
In this movement of the cloud;
And in this gentle wind turning wild.
<u>Poem by Olatubosun David</u>

Olatubosun David is a Nigeria writer and poet. He is a member of PEN, Nigeria Centre. A graduate of Rufus Giwa Polytechnic, Owo, Ondo State, currently works in Achievers University, Owo. Ondo State, Nigeria. He is on Twitter @davidolatubosun and Instagram @olatubosundavid and Facebook: facebook.com/ Tubotech.

17. The Bend On The River

It was along the bend on the diminutive river,
Shaded by tropical flora and lush greens,
That I sat contemplating about life, people and things as e'er,
With only the gurgling sound of water to stoke my dreams .
The cool breeze wafting through the palms calmed my senses,
The myriad fragrances of nature soothed my soul,
As extemporaneous poesy came gushing in torrents,
And my thoughts were flowing so positive and ne'er afoul.
The chirping of crickets and the cooing of a cuckoo,
The pristine music and melodies of nature,
Drummed on my ears in a pleasant staccato,
And Lo Behold! ne'er did I feel more one with the creator.
Forests, sunshine, a pristine brook and bright blue sky,
Is this real and perceptible or just a puissant fantasy!!
Poem by <u>ARUN HARIHARAN</u>

Arun Hariharan a.k.a Harry, is an Indian Army veteran who switched over to a Corporate career post his military service. A compulsive traveller, photographer, author, poet and history buff- he's always loved exploring the unexplored. Arun's collection of Short Stories titled "A Baker's Dozen- 13 Chilling Indian Tales of Macabre" which incorporated three of his passions - travel, history and exploring local legends-was published in October 2021.

18. Beloved Dandelions

Oh dandelion
I love to watch you grow
From yellow bud
to golden flower
you change yourself
each coming hour
Children pick you
for their mothers
who receive them
as if they are a rose bouquet
As you grow old
your hoary heads
are blown into the wind
as your seeds drift
down into the earth
I know you'll grow again.
Poem by Ruth M. Martz
_BIO:__A poet and She does all kinds of crafts, Spinning wool ,_
knitting etc.

19. My postgraduate pillars

It all started just like that one fine morning,

Have to wake up early mornings,

Go to a new place,

Meeting new people,

To obey rules,

To do what is commanded,

With increasing days , increasing pressure !

There came my saviors !!

Sweethearts ,darlings who made me to forget all my frustrations ,

Making my days beautiful day by day !!

My brotherly figure made my posting better and finer ,

Supporting me no matter I am right or wrong,

encouraging me when I am down,

Teaching me when I am wrong ,

Questioning me when I am going back .

Taking part in both ups and down..

You were my guide, brother ,teacher !

Thank you my saviors !!

Poem by Nishanthini Iniyan

BIO: *Author's name is Dr.Nishanthini, who has done her postgraduation in Prosthodontics . He has passion in writting .*

20. Wayfaring Dandelion Seeds

i hastily close my eyes; i take a breath
and blow the seeds off a dandelion—
wayfaring bristles journey the breeze
across yellow field, and leave behind
florets grasping on stems against flight.
frail cotton wishes crumble away.
uplifting wind briskly send me away
into the horizon by a simple breath;
as seeds shed sporeful veils, my flight
says goodbye to the yellow dandelions
which are still swaying happily behind
me—catching slightly by the breeze.
from a blow, the tufty seeds breezily
tip along the trails and tumble away
to open plots, but half-hidden behind
looming bushes from the frigid breath—
setting with other yellow dandelions
instead of roaming in this long flight—
because teetering is an arduous flight.
there are moments along this breezy

whisper when dozing deep dandelions
forget the airy tufts that went away.
many partings leave seeds breathless
as they wander—a few steps behind—
through with only few glances behind
them before they descend their flight.
so i take a stroll with a tired breath;
i catch the hazy seeds in the breeze,
while they wistfully snowflake away—
someday to bud their own dandelions.
for now, they pass by the dandelions
to follow a faint draft, leaving behind
the yellow field for new land far away.
they take wishes with them in flight,
only enough to ride the brief breeze—
as i once again take in a heavy breath.
i release a sigh; a dandelion takes flight
and tosses in the breeze. i leave behind
the florets that took my breath away.

Poem by Andrew Huang

Andrew Huang, also known as Change, has been writing poetry since high school when he first discovered spoken word poetry in an after school program. During that time, he participated in teen performances, such as the annual Youth Speak Poetry Slam. Change continued his passion for poetry writing by in college by enrolling in English courses and writing workshops. He took a brief pause in his literary pursuit due to the increase loads of school work, as well as discovering his passion for dancing. Due to the pandemic, he has rekindled his passion for the literary art, and has since refining his craft through form experimentation and storytelling exploration. He has started an international event in 2022 called World Poetry Symposium as a way to celebrate April National Poetry Month.

21. Search

Death crawled in with a phone call.
With four words he announced
His Victory!
The castle of cards pulverized.
Childhood pages made the pyre,
Where vintage memories are burning.
Pieces of fun, drops of moments,
Flashing before my eyes,
Tears are now eye dwellers.
With a cacophonous mind and blurred sight
I'm searching my brother in
Handful of ashes!
Poem by SANHITA SINHA

Sanhita Sinha, born & brought up in Tripura, is a teacher, a bilingual poet. Her poems were published in different prestigious national and international anthologies, journals & magazines. Her first book " SILENT BYSTANDER" was published in 2020 & second book " KATHA ROOP KATHA "(a collection of her Bengali poems) was published in 2022 and many other works are in the pipeline. Sanhita's works were published in IFLAC peace anthology, POESIA 2021, organised by Institute of Linguistics of the Russian Academy of science, Balmont foundation , Moscow poetry Biennale & Poets' circle Greece. She was also a contributing poet of " The National Indie Excellence Awards 2021 finalist book, THE KALI PROJECT : INVOKING THE GODDESS WITHIN ". BANGA

BANDHU SMARAK GRANTHA on Banga Bandhu Sheikh Mujibur Rahman. MAHATMA A LIVING LEGEND on Mohandas Karamchand Gandhi. A HAIKU TREASURY of her haiku poems, and many more. Along with Bengali and English her poems were translated in Russian language as well. As an editor, subtitler Sanhita worked in three short films of reknowned Bahubhuj production, two of them won several prizes.As a lyricist also she has earned love by the music lovers. She also has succeessfully organised poetry-painting exhibition with her poems & paintings. Apart from writing, as an elocutionist , as an actor she is actively engaged in different cultural activities. Along with stage she is a regular artist of Television and All India Radio,Agartala too. Sanhita is also a winner of CCRT national scholarship in drama and recently she was honored by the "SAHITYA PATA KAZI NAZRUL ISLAM BIRTH ANNIVERSARY AWARD 2022"

22. Weeds Are Beautiful Too

Surreal wisps scattered -
in the breath of final moments
as the gentle breeze of life
extinguishes heartbeats that fluttered,
fluttered and raced -
throbbed,
raced and throbbed
crushed,
crushed underfoot
then was no more.
"Weeds are beautiful too", he said
as he departed
to which she replied,
"Roses have thorns".
Poem by Bilkis Moola

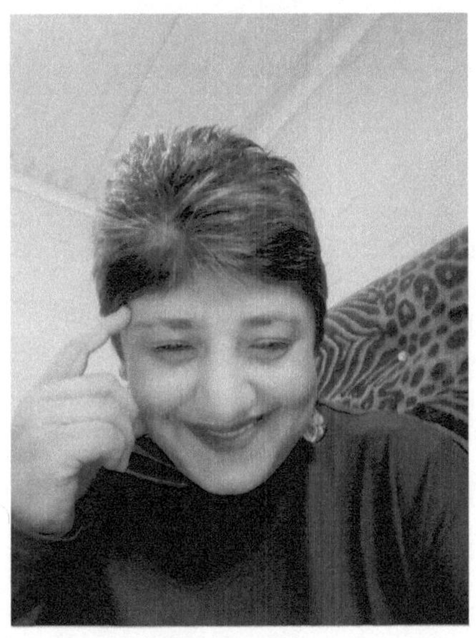

Bilkis Moola's journey as a poet commenced with the publication of her first collection of poems, "Wounds and Wings:.A Lyrical Salve Through Metaphor". Her second collection of poetry, "Ebb and Flow of Love"was freshly launched in 2020. She has evolved into a voice that has been translated into Spanish, Hindi, French and Polish with her poems globally received in poetry magazines , reviews and journals as well as as virtual poetry reading platforms. Her third contribution to the poetic arena is "Footsteps in Shadows", published and launched in 2022. A poet from South Africa, Bilkis Moola is a Senior Education Specialists.

23. That Bloody War

When a snake is in the meadow, the shades you
Long are there, but are
Unreachable.
Betrayals are more bitter then.
You feel lonely, deserted, battered.
Remember, you are not a mere
person, but an entity
Spread about the dust and souls
as you tread, like
A quantum packet of existence.
Lives are entangled, and some are
Tied together with knots
Deep within.
This fight didn't have to be
So sanguine, painful and long.
But you cannot let go of
A shadow that
Is rooted in your flesh, citing
Logic and sense.

<u>Poem by Fariel Shafee</u>

<u>BIO:</u> *The author has degrees in science, but enjoys writing. She has published poems in Kritya, The Literary Nest, Millers Pond* *etc. url: http://fshafee.wixsite.com/farielsart*

24. Never Stop

Let the tones of gladness ring
Clear as song of birds of spring.
Don't be scared of problems,
play them as game
Your good qualities will bring you
a lot of fame.
One angry moment often does
What we repent for years,
It works the wrong we made right
By sorrow or by tears.
Today the skies are clear and blue
Tomorrow clouds may come in view
Yesterday was not for you, Do it now.
If there comes water ,
we should stop and drink
Amongst the rock one cannot stop and think.
It doesn't matter if fights were lost
Someday you'll win too;
And that day will come fast
This is something true.
Losing hope is not the work of man,
To work hard is the aim of man.

No matter whom or what you are
You surely can win your strife;
Though at times results are sour
You will have a good life.
Nothing is impossible, just use your brain
Once it is on track, it runs fast as train.
Poem by _AFRAH SADIQA S S_

Afrah Sadiqa. S. S is a Dental student of Dr.M.G.R University,
Chennai. She is passionate towards academics and extra-
curricular activities. She has an optimistic nature and believes in
achieving her dreams.

25. Deromantica

When did your heart froze in the icy skate rink?
I actually thought this love flaming like summer
would burn the sorrow down to the pithole?
Even my voice can make the ocean full bloom back to blue
or will the clouds make it wither
and its petals marched down the ocean?
I don't wanna marry the umbrella because I'm not the rain
I will just do anything to let the wind sweep your anger towards
the cliff
I will not let the wings of the sky cover you, my masterpiece.
Thunder, thunder, I beg you, I beg you!
Don't struck me by your intense wrath!
I wouldn't lose my masterpiece in the middle of fog
or will I lost it?
Will I really lost you?
<u>Poem by Jhenson Tyrone Villena</u>

Jhenson Tyrone Villena hails from the country of the Philippines. A certified introvert who is a bookworm. He is currently exploring the world of literature specifically poem writing and story writing.

26. A Whisper

O sky why so? I always cried as I was tired of trying;
O earth why so? I always yelled as I was laid upon knees;
O wind why so? I always halted by the haunting life;
My complaining nature, nurtured my weakness with
dissatisfaction.
Full of confusion to hustle with struggling world to smuggle the
smile which I never owed.
Bowed to down the weight which weighed more not to low,
A whisper changed everything was as loud as thunder!!
Heart beats pumped so heavy to give tension of hypertension;
Moment to be cherished not spring or autumn but the Almighty
spent!!!
Now the air blows to wind up the negative thoughts;
The earths harvests with a new hope;
The sky covers the black clouds to blank it up;
A new man a new era!
A new sail of sensation!
To trench up the dark deeds!
Tears still flows even the frequency is more, but won't tear now!
The body screams even louder, but won't breach now!
Life is not a play of some sort of soft clay, that Kintsugi will
help,,

A small split will bury up the whole life...
The depression once was a dot now became global;
The world of fake smile is getting submerged with its own
polluted thoughts.
I wonder, I wonder !
How the creatures are howling with pain of insecurity and
abomination...
A step towards light is enough to head up,
Give space to air to pace up the layer of humanity,
O man, O man...
Why don't you step out of your circle to globe of reality;
A little change is enough to move the noise which made all deaf!
I will take off my step of pride to jump in humble path...
I will loosen up the grudges to free enmity...
You too give try...
Let's try for regeneration not of repair as scars always leaves
mark!
Let's seek a brighter hue in this planet of blue...
Poem by Bhavya M Bhaskaran

BIO: *Bhavya is a simple girl, who lives a simple life. She is not Wordsworth or R Bond but likes to use words to express aspects.*

27. Why did we grow up?

Why did we grow up?
To walk miles,
forgetting about smiles?
How happiness
And social media had no connection
Why did we grow up?
Only to experience
Failures and rejections?
Singing give me some sunshine
With friends was fun.
But now when the lyrics hit you hard
You can no more have fun singing it.
Yeah, so why did we grow up?
Poem by Shravani Prakashchandra

She is Shravani Prakashchandra, she's completed her 12th grade. She wants to pursue a degree in psychology. You could read her poems in anthologies; Enchantments and Mystic beauty of love. Her favorite poets are Lang Leav, Rupi Kaur and Robert Frost. You could connect with her on Instagram @shrav._z

28. After The Pandemic

*A new day is dawning when the world
will sing and dance, and celebrate
the end of the global pandemic.*

*Friends will meet face to face,
grandparents will hug their grandchildren,
businesses will reopen their doors,
actors and singers returning to the stage
and screen.*

*Feel the cool breeze blowing in your hair,
book that long awaited holiday,
put on your dancing shoes and
greet the morning light!*
Poem by LaVern Spencer McCarthy

LaVern Spencer McCarthy has published six books of poetry and four books of short stories. She is a life member of Poetry Society Of Texas. Her work has appeared in Poetry Society of Texas, Book Of The Year, Encore, Visions International, Home Life Magazine, Cappers and manyu anthologies. She resides in Blair Oklahoma.

29. Follow me

I give you a secret sign, follow the white rabbit.
My tattoo on my shoulder speaks.
Yes, I forgot, we are not in the Matrix movie.
I want you to be my companion,
but you don't know how to read signs
set by the Universe
through numbers and in the child's speech.
There is a celestial draftsman whose pen prints horoscope signs.
It's all as clear as the future,
in response to prayer.
But instead of watching,
you sleep and dream of me in a silk nightgown,
and you don't realize I'm warm on a hot night,
not to provoke your senses.
I give you the way you walk without material desires
and to head to the Himalayas
where we will look with different eyes.
We will dive into the mountain of snow,
in whose interior there is a world of abundance.
Close your eyes and follow me.
I'll take you, companion,
when you learn that tattoos speak,

when you know the signs written in gold pen,
we will not need a body of earth.
Follow me, I'll take you to the abundance of dreams come true.
And when you step in there, you won't want to go back,
but he wanted it first.
Poem by Maja Milojković

*Maja Milojković was born in 1975 in Zaječar, Serbia and lives
and works in Denmark. She is a person to whom, as a
laboratory assistant from an early age, Leonardo da Vinci's
statement "Painting is poetry that can be seen, and poetry is*

painting that can be heard" is circulating through the blood. That's why she started to use feathers and a brush and began to reveal the world and herself to them. As a poet, she is represented in numerous domestic and foreign literary newspapers, anthologies and electronic media, and some of her songs can be found on YouTube. Many of her poems have been translated into English, Hungarian and Bulgarian due to the need of foreign readers. "Trees of Desire" is her second collection of poems in preparation, which is preceded by the book of poems "Moon Circle". She is a member of the International Society of Writers and Artists "Mountain Views" in Montenegro

30. Journey

It all started with crush at first sight
Continued with hints
From working all together
To connecting forever

.

Love started later
It was getting all better
Falling for her was never a choice
It was all destiny falling for her eyes, her voice.

.

Days continued, till the time comes
She started getting irritated
Started all hiding
I been the understanding
She created all worse
Those wasn't the period mood swing
But a bell ring for someone else entering in.

.

Multiple secrets took place
Can't understand how to trace
Started ignoring the fact
Imagining the past

It was just money who theft her
Caught her red handed
Instead of apologize, she started a scene
At last I get all dirty and she left with a chit clean.

.

Transformation took place
Changed from sweet to sour
Just a random guy to well known hack
Self transformation been to an extent
At this point there's no turning back.
<u>Poem by Aayush Aggarwal</u>

Aayush Aggarwal is an incurable introvert who find peace in
spending times with loved ones or in solitude. He's unimaginable
tall boy with fun loving attitude, who believes in living life
today cz may be "kal Ho Na Ho". The writing wasn't a lifestyle

or passion for him unless he found someone or something to connect with. He's not a reader but a book itself with some dark and some white pages. He's wanderer too. His dream is to explore all the deepest and darkest mysteries of world because he's mystery in himself. Contact via; Instagram: @iaayushaggarwal

31. Get Over Thinking

Ever felt like 19 tabs being open at once???

Kept few decisions unmade, you don't even know ever since??

Seen the watch couple times in a single minute???

Yet couldn't figure out the time, when actually asked for it???

Always have to keep the songs playing in ears???

Just to prevent those waves of thoughts from drowning the mind of yours???

Every simple decision feels like a big chore,

Every small chore resting heavy like a burden,

Every single burden holding you down like a million ton??? Ever felt that???

If you can relate,

and your mind is currently starting anew debate....

Lol, Let's just say congratulation!!!

We all mastered the art of overthinking and procastination!!!

Well others might think iam exhausted without doing anything much....

Trust me. Iam running miles in mind, not that easy to explain as such.

Do I wanna get over this overthinking??

Yes.

Do I also enjoy being myself and finding problem for every solution??

Hell yes!!

Maybe one day...I'll enjoy the peace of mind like the deep dark

ocean.

But until then... let me vibe to my own chaotic waves of

emotions.

Poem by Nivedha Somasundharam

She is a Doctor (to be), treating souls through prescribing doses of

poems.

32. When mama came into my room

Shock upon shock, she angrily talked
Where is your manner, my boy?
Do you need some class?
Books and pens, a mug and a cello-tape,
Lying on the floor, when I open the door.
Are you a monkey?
Nah! Even a monkey has a brain more.
And what's that....?
Paper wrappers and a calculator too
Even a pig will not do like you.
Where is your manner, boy?
And don't you have a brain?
Reminder for you this time!
But I will crush you if I see that again.
This is heartbreaking news of the last week;
Is my mother only the one on earth who speaks?

Poem by Suk Raj Darjee

BIO: Suk Raj Darjee is a budding bard born in 2002, in the holy Himalayan country of Bhutan. To date, he has been featured in national TV news, newspapers, journals, websites,

MUHAMED FARHAAN

has been co-author of more than 20 anthologies, and appreciated by numerous global literary platforms.

• 71 •

33. I Bleed on paper

I Spread the Silent Words on Paper
I Bleed on the Paper with Serenity
Mix them with the Colors of Nature
I Spread them like stars in the sky
I throw the Words of Black and White
I Spread them in meaningful colors
I Bleed on the Paper with the Tears
I Spread them like a Fragrance in the sky
I just Bleed on the Paper
With the helplessness in the eyes
Poem by Neelam Lashari

Neelam Lashari an Author and a Bilingual Poet. She is in the writing field for the last eight years as it gives her pleasure to write her heart out. On the other hand, she has her feet in freelancing which, enhances her writing abilities, and insists her to help people in the field of writing. She is the author of the book named "The Comfort of Hardship". Moreover, she is a co-author of 81 international books and countless books are in pipeline. She throws the ink on canvas to represent the feelings and emotions of the masses through touchy words. Neelam belongs to Lahore, Pakistan. Her official account is voiceofsoul_by_neelamlashari

34. Thoughts

"*A beautiful sparkling ray of light, shining even through at dim lights, as passing through the deep and dark forests it is becoming more and more bright. Never felt that the nature shines more bright even in the small sparking light. Just want to be with the nature and enjoy each and every blissful moments...*"

"*It is a pleasant and a beautiful evening, never expected that one evening may change my whole life so beautiful. Met such a an amazing person with a pure soul of love, laughter and all the emotions. Turning out each and every normal day to a special and memorable day. May this beautiful relationship lasts forever with many more beautiful memories and many cute moments. Let me be your little munchkin forever..*"

Poem by Sai Sravanthi

BIO: *Sai Sravanthi is from Andhra Pradesh. She is a wonderful writer. Her Thoughts on writing the quotes are very expressive and very passionate about in writing. She is an ambivert girl. Her thoughts are so expressive and unique. You can take a look at her writings on Instagram : @_creative_thoughts_143*

35. I Keep Quiet

I keep quiet because I love you;
Not because I don't have voice.
I keep quiet because you know my silence,
Then why should I make noise?
I keep quiet drinking a sea tears
Hiding a wounded broken heart,
Because I know I can't live
Without my soul's part.
I keep quiet devouring my fiery anger
Because you are the one only whom I care,
I keep quiet because I have fear
To loss the bonding that's rare.
I keep quiet getting hurt myself
Than to hurt you whom I love the most,
I keep quiet for my own sake
To save my love at any cost
<u>Poem by Eity Mithila</u>

Eity Mithila is a young poetess who was born in 6 February in Bangladesh.She obtained her Masters degree in English literature from Begum Bodrunnesa Government Girls' College under Dhaka University.Composing poetry is her passion and genres in which she is more interested are spiritual and love poetry. Moreover,she achieved awards and certificates from different international literary platforms and her poems have been published in different anthologies of different countries.

Follow As23

@anonymoussoul23